EARLENE TORRES

Escape to Guam USA

(Nostalgic Reflections of an Islander Far From Home)

This book was professionally typeset on Reedsy.
Find out more at reedsy.com

To My son Nicholas who inspires me to Dream Big
May your Heart lead you to do great things,
to love God and yourself
each Day.

Contents

1

Introduction

"*H*afa Adai!" That is a greeting in Guam as - Welcome/Hello/How Are You? My name is Earlene B. Torres. I was born and raised on the island of Guam, the largest of the Southern Marianas islands, within Micronesia in the Western Pacific Ocean. I am a product of a very proud culture of islanders. If you imagine the likes of the Disney character "Moana" and her people's roots embedded with ancestors, superstitions and their love of land and sea - you get the gist of who I am.

Sadly, I am not living proof of where I am today compared to where I came from. I currently live in a landlocked area in Central California. I went off to have an adventure to reunite with off-island relatives when I was eighteen, thinking I would return within the year. It's now 2022 and I am still far from home for the last 43 years! Not an ocean or palm tree in sight! But *"why are you writing this book"* - you ask?

Because I know out there, other Guamanians are also living abroad, doing whatever the reason was they left home to do. They are also thinking and believing they will return home one day. Yet, time passes and their heart always calls to mind what and whom they left behind. Writing this book is a promise to myself that I will go back and reclaim my home, not just visit. So in the meantime - I will share stories and experiences that will help all of us living abroad, connect with Guam in all its charm and give us even more of a conviction to return home for good. So now that you know my reason, let us get started with a few trivial facts.

Guam is roughly 125 square miles, with a population of 168,783 at the last census of 2020. It is the westernmost territory of the United States. Its capital is "Hagatna" (pronounced ha-got-nya). Due to its location on the opposite side of the International Date Line, Guam is 17 hours ahead of the western coast of the United States. Guam's famous claim is a motto seen in all our tourism and mass media publications: "Where America's Day Begins."

Local residents and natives fondly refer to the island as "The Rock". We know it only shows up as a tiny "dot" marker on the global map. But this tiny "rock" holds a lot of special qualities for explorers and visitors once they have experienced taking a trip or vacation in Guam. This Rock is also a very convenient " tropical getaway" destination for weddings, honeymoons, educators, marine biologists, and world-class surfers. It is approximately a three to four-hour plane ride from Japan, the Philippines, and Australia. For those wanting an exotic island locale experience in Oceania, there is a saving on time and airfare going to Guam versus flying all the way to Hawaii in the Pacific.

An endless golden sunset to drive home by

These are the general tidbits about Guam you would find on a surface level. I am here to share with you my perspective, a native who was born and raised here pretty much up until the day I left at the age of 19. Just to start off, I will be using frequent terms like "Chamoru" or 'Chamorro' -the native people and "language tongue" of Guam. "Brown" - a modern slang term islanders call each other as an endearment depicted by our skin color. You may hear teenagers of today use "bruh" when referring to their "besties" or friends in America. Same thing. LOL! The time away may have been decades in my case, but the memories in my mind's eye are just like yesterday. I hope you enjoy my sense of humor.

2

The 671 - Not Just An Area Code

As I have mentioned, Guam is a U.S. Territory. Therefore, people from the Mainland (the USA - as referred to by Guam residents), can dial directly to the island with the area code 671. This is how it is today. But for my life as a child of yesteryear, we did not have telephones. Okay, correction - most "households" did not have phones installed in Guam because it was not a standard utility. We're talking back to the 1960s, early 70s until urban renewal housing came about. We lived as we did with our neighbors being more like family and not strangers. We can just go over to each other's house and socialize on the porch, by the outside kitchen or just about anywhere we can find shade and some refreshments. All initiated by a holler or yell to come out. Unless no one was home, you pretty much will get a response when a head pops out the open door or window. It doesn't take much to get people to gather around each other's yard or driveway, even in the middle of the street. We usually share gossip, betel nut (a local "edible" favorite) and perhaps a can of soda (for kids) and beer or "tuba" (spirit moonshine made from coconut tree sap) for the adults.

Guamanians identify with the numbers 671 printed on t-shirts, auto decals, and stickers blatantly printed over the island map of Guam, in its design. As an alternative design, 671 is also printed with the revered Chamoru Chief Kepuha (also spelled Quipuha - key-poo-ha). His image was a visual way of showing our pride in our heritage. It's also a "call signal" to natives living abroad that someone wearing or displaying 671 is from their island home and the reaction is to invite him or her into the conversation - "Hey Brown!" or "Hafa Adai!" It's not a guarantee that they will be natives. But if they have lived on Guam for a time, we tend to embrace them as honorary Guamanians. But yes, being brown has its meaningful assertions.

Growing up "Brown"

We don't take it personally as a negative, using this term for our skin color. It is way better than being called "Gook" as depicted in slang used in television media or by prejudiced outsiders deferring to "little brown people". We love that we don't burn easily in the hot tropical sun, as we are a range of shades from (lightest)- cafe Au lait, to latte, to coffee, to chocolate (darkest) because we are a blend of Spanish and "Austronesian" traits, given our historical past and our region of Micronesia. Our tan gets better as we soak in the natural sunlight; we are practically golden in our glow when we glam up with bright colors in our swimwear or dress up in colorful floral prints. Ladies - get that hot pink lipstick out and nail polish - we sparkle like cotton candy when paired up against our skin tone! Work that "Brown" to its fullest!

We take "Brown" as an endearment and being inclusive like a brother hood. Guamanians are very loyal and family oriented. If you ever find yourself stranded with a dead car battery, whether on the side of the road or in the parking lot of a local store or plaza, if the hood is up - the browns come over to check if you need help. You may want to pay them for their kindness after fixing your mechanical issue or dilemma. More than likely, they won't accept money, but if you offer to buy them a beer - you just became a Brown in their eyes. After a few swigs and some introductions, don't be surprised if they ask for your full name, then begin to mentally check if you may be a relative once they hear your last name. You can see them methodically connecting the dots as they ask if you know this person or that person, or if you went to school here or there and what village did you live or are originally from. I hope this habit of "trace ancestry" has not fallen away over the years since I left Guam. You could build your own extended family and add to a network of "friends like family" just by this practice. Multi-level marketers can't compete with this team building method. LOL!

Catholicism and the Fear of God "Per Nana"

Okay - few background facts before I get started on this subtopic. Ferdinand Magellan, the Portuguese explorer who circumnavigated the globe on Spanish expeditions is officially recognized as the one who put Guam and the Marianas Islands on the map. He claimed the island for Spain and with it came the Jesuit Priests who were also trying to bring Christianity to all new lands brought under the Spanish throne. The Jesuits who arrived in Guam were greeted by Chief Kepuha. Through their teachings of God and a higher being, Chief Kepuha became the first to be baptized a Catholic and the rest followed. So religion and going to church became a staple in just about the majority of the island's population. It would seem out of the ordinary if you didn't know how to pray or have religious statues and rosaries within your household.

My primary introduction to religion came from my Nana (my paternal grandmother). Nana always made us pray before meals, practiced saying the rosary, and held us accountable to observing Lent season (meatless Fridays) with the Holy Week affirmations before Easter Sunday. She instilled in us, our knowledge of the immense power of the All-Mighty. On that note, Nana also taught us not to "lie, steal or misbehave" because God was everywhere and would expose our crimes. We would be punished for being sinners and our souls would burn eternally in purgatory. I used to imagine as a child that the religious pictures or statues around Nana's house made it more believable that we were being "watched" in her absence from the room. That painting of the Last Supper told me that Jesus and his twelve apostles were not short of being "witnesses" to any "sins" we were committing behind Nana's back.

I was too scared to "lie" and the thought of "hell and the burning fires of purgatory" per Nana's inquisition, gave me plenty of reasons not to be "bad". I would try to walk the straight and narrow line and be the "good Catholic girl" she would be proud of, but it wasn't an easy road. Temptations were everywhere in the form of "fitting in" at school. Did I mention that I also went to Catholic school? Talk about "peer pressure" with Nuns around campus to boot. Our uniforms were like prison garments holding us captive to religious standards. We are not allowed to have our skirt hem above the knee nor could we wear bright nail polish, makeup, or dangling earrings. If we did, it would cheapen us in the eyes of the Lord, as we would be compared to Jezebel, a harlot in the bible. She was a "sinner."

As I grew up, I developed an understanding that Nana's way of teaching us about the Catholic faith was more a "good" versus "bad" upbringing. It was also her way of controlling our morals and thought process. She was truly preparing us to become conscientious responsible teenagers and adults. Sundays are a way of celebrating our devotion and faith to God (and it also gave us a chance to connect with relatives and friends in attendance). Living out here in the states, I still attend mass and practice my Catholic faith. Though I do have a circle of friends and acquaintances, I still miss meeting up with relatives after services. It's been a little isolating for me as I get older. But thanks to Nana, I have a deeper appreciation for the word of the Lord. I reflect upon the scriptures and feel its connection to how she viewed the world in her advanced years. I live alone with my son in Central CA without immediate family. But I never once thought I was totally on my own. God and Jesus were with me and no matter what, I could get through anything.

Without even realizing it, I applied the same foundation of faith with my son. He was baptized and also attended a Catholic school that had both Nuns and Priest as part of campus life with our parish church next door. He is my miracle child. An amazing gift from God after years of hardship and a tearful journey of struggling through infertility. But against all odds, at the age of 41, I gave birth to my son, naturally, healthy and without any complications. Secretly, I think God sent me my blessing, but I wouldn't put it past me to think Nana was also there at His side, smiling along on that day. She's still "watching" me from Heaven - another Angel who started out putting the "Fear of God" in me, only to later embrace Him wholeheartedly. That was truly Nana's gift and her legacy to me. Thank you Nana - you are always in my daily prayers!

3

Customs from History and Modern Influences

pain and Catholicism

S Our island was first discovered by Portuguese explorer Ferdinand Magellan who actually sailed for Spain, over 500 years ago in 1521. His Spanish Galleon ships found Guam to be the ideal stop along the Spain - Manila trade routes. Ferdinand Magellan, a Catholic, also opened the gates to the arrival of Jesuit Priests. The natives were labeled "Chamorro" (Chamoru) by the priests as it described the masculine native like Chief Kepuha as "scantily clad, with short, shaven hair, cropped closely to the scalp." The Jesuits put into place the structures of colonization, with small groupings of huts that normally had a church in the center of what was designated as "villages". Religion and Christianity was a foremost focal point of the Jesuits and their presence in Guam. Magellan did not genuinely have any interest in Guam and its natives. He held himself in high regard, viewing the people as savages or heathens and at times, due to their unbridled curiosity,

9

took things from the ships that were docked a few miles of the bay closest to the island. He called Guam "Isla de Ladrones" - island of thieves. He did not stay on to oversee the colonization of Guam, leaving that task mostly to the priests. But years later, trouble came in the form of a ranking Jesuit Priest's death. The Jesuit was killed for secretly baptizing a child of the ruling Chief Matapang. Chief Matapang was angered once the deception came to light and had the priest killed. This caused the Spaniards to return and imposed military installation to prevent any further uprisings.

Years of occupancy brought about the intermingling of Spanish influences in the form of family surnames, language adaptation, food staples and even clothing. The women wore white cotton undergarments with mesh overlays of embroidered floral and beaded designs with arched, puffed sleeves in the style Spanish women wore. This dress or formal clothing style is called a "Mestiza".

Usually, my grandmother and the ancestors before her, would wear these as formal wear to a party or social event as well as to Sunday mass. Nana had a variety of these dresses in all the colors of the rainbow. She wore her hair up in a bun and headwear was usually covered with a lace material, much like the mantillas worn by the "duennas" you would see in a Spanish themed movie. A lot of terms in our native "tongue or dialect" has Latin-based roots.

When I was in school, I took Spanish as a foreign language subject. But to my surprise, it was revealing that often, the connection between our two worlds was very much the same as Spanish terms were used in the Chamorro dialect we spoke. The only difference is, that the Chamorro tongue would "butcher" the Spanish words in pronunciation. For example, "verde" is "bede"(bet-dee) and "color" is "colot". It was not as foreign as I expected it to be - the joke was on me! Needless to say, in the end, the study of Spanish has helped me learn to apply it in my travels away from Guam.

Out here in California, I easily got addicted to Hispanic Novelas (soap operas) and made fast friends with my Spanish-speaking colleagues and within Hispanic community settings. My father's family are direct descendants of Spaniards from the past, thus our surname is Spanish. Torres is defined as "towers". Many Chamorros have descended from Spaniards as well.

When I think back to the remnants of Spanish rule in Guam, I think of Fort Soledad, the Spanish outpost placed high atop one side of the hills that surround the waterway into Umatac Bay. The port entry where the Spanish galleons sailed with Magellan and the Jesuits. Soledad in English is defined as "solitude" or "solitary" and Fort Soledad, high above the bay, truly gives you the feeling of being alone and in isolation. A soldier was posted there to be on lookout watch towards the ocean for any incoming ships and to relay any sightings to the authorities ahead, just in case unfriendly visitors (such as pirates) came calling.

As for the poor Jesuit Priest who was slain? He has been revered as a "martyr" and his legacy lives on - a church in his name and a beach commemorating his point of death - Padre San Vitores. Not far from Tumon Bay is Padre San Vitores beach.

But you know, out here in the states, most people assume that if your last name is Hispanic or Latin-based, you are quickly placed on the Hispanic mailing list and marketing offers. I often receive Spanish programming discounts from my local cable and utilities provider. Little did these agencies know that I may be Brown and have a Spanish surname, but am a transplant and a Pacific Islander from Guam. There I go again with the 671 mentality!

Japan and World War II

Now it is fair to say that Guam continues to be at the crosswinds, or rather crossfire, of ruling countries of power. We definitely did not expect to be in the way of any plan to be a part of World War II. This one hit "home" in a much personal way for me. My parents, both young children at the time of the Pearl Harbor bombing in 1941, quickly found themselves and their families thrown into the Japanese vision of taking the battle overseas on the way to invading the United States by targeting Pearl Harbor. My mom is originally from the Northern Marianas island of Saipan. My dad is from Guam, but the whole archipelago of islands known collectively as The Marianas Islands, were invaded by the Japanese under the cover of darkness right before the early morning dawn on December 8, 1941. Remember, these islands are on the opposite side of the International Date Line, so despite the distance between us and Hawaii, there were 17 hours of war and capture that took place 17 hours ahead of the arrival of the Imperial Fleet and Japanese Fighter Planes on the horizon outside Pearl Harbor.

My parents have re-told their recollections of living under Japanese rule for many years. The Imperial Army and takeover in the Marianas was swift and not resisted. It became a matter of survival, having witnessed people being murdered by beheading from samurai swords or stabbing from the tip of a bayonet blade at the end of a rifle. My mom's family and other relatives have recalled hiding in the hills within caves. My dad remembers how he, as a young boy of ten hauled rocks and bags of sand and gravel, along with other males, to build the runways for the Japanese planes to land. It was a dark time in our history, but they managed to survive in their respective islands and lived to see the day when US troops rescued the Marianas from Japan's rule. We continue to celebrate that freedom, known as "Liberation Day" every 21st of July. Japan lost the battle after the nuclear bomb devastated the town of Hiroshima by the US. The nearby island of Tinian actually played a big part in this historical event. It was from Tinian, where the famous "Enola Gay" airplane flew out to deliver the first atomic/nuclear bomb used in war. There are still remnants from the war in the jungle "boonies" of Guam and the rest of the Marianas Islands. Fort Apugan (ah-pooh-gun) still displays the three cannons used in ground to air warfare. We even had a living historical figure during my lifetime.

When I was in sixth grade, my class took a field trip to a popular waterfall located within the central hills of Guam, known as Talafofo Falls. Just months before, a Japanese soldier by the name of Sgt. Shoichi Yokoi, was discovered to be living in a cave hidden from sight by the waterfall. The year was 1972; 28 years after the end of WWII and he stayed hidden, with the belief that he would one day be rescued by his comrades. In local papers, he was called "the Last Japanese Straggler". It was a remarkable, almost unbelievable story of the human spirit and the will to survive on his own, all those years alone in that cave. He was returned to Japan as a hero, but accounts of his life from his nephew, told of return visits to Guam with his wife when possible and he would go to the cave that became his "lost" home. He passed away in 1997, but is honored fondly by Guamanians to this day. Sgt. Yokoi's name is still painted on the waterfall's entry marker as part of a main tourist attraction. A woven fishing basket that he constructed from palm fronds to catch eels in the river for food, is displayed in a local museum depicting his ingenuity in surviving the wild. May I mention that we did undergo a second "Japanese invasion" - this time in the form of tourism? Many Japanese tourists come to Guam to either enjoy the island's attractions or have a tropical wedding experience. Yet, shortly after Yokoi's discovery, a portion of Japanese tourists were an influx of relatives of the Empire's fallen troops. They came mostly to pay respects at a shrine memorial in honor of loved ones whose bodies never returned home and were last known to be in Guam when the war ended.

American Infused - A United States Territory

We became a U.S. Territory at the end of the war, officially by the "Organic Act of 1950". Once Uncle Sam freed us from Japanese rule at the end of World War II, it became evident that strategically, we were the first line of defense to protect future invasions on the shores of America. Guam was immediately a ground for military installations, the Air Force, and the Navy. Military bases became a part of our landscape at both the north and south ends of the island. My parents both became civil servants - Mom worked at Andersen Airforce Base, the home of the B52s and the heavyweight C41 transport. Dad worked in the U.S. Navy Public Works, where all documentation of government services regarding the land and navigational maps of the surrounding Pacific Ocean were cataloged and archived for military resources and strategic planning. During the years of growing up, our lifestyle mimicked the all-American dream - television programming came from Los Angeles California, and our infrastructure mirrored governing laws the same. We have the same seat belt law enforced in Guam as they do in California. Our schools are the same public school system as the mainland, with

English textbooks and scholastic programs.

I always dreamed one day I would leave the Rock to head out to America where excitement and all things red-white-and blue were calling me. I used to plan my Saturday television watching in this order and purpose. At around 10a.m. I turned on American Bandstand with Dick Clark, so I could get a look at the latest fashion clothing worn by American teens. At 11 a.m., I continued to watch "Soul Train " with Don Cornelius so I could tap into the boogie music and learn the awesome dance moves. I used to imagine I would make it down that "Soul Train Express Line " where people would come down the center of two lines of dancers, showing their best steps or moves. If I was good with grades and earned a little "cash" for my effort, I would use my money to go to Island Records in Mangilao and spend it on either 45- vinyl singles or 33 RPM full Albums ranked by Kasey Kasem's American Top 40 Hit chart. I also couldn't forget when fast-food chains came to the island. Did you know that on June 10, 1971, the first McDonald's on Guam in Tamuning village opened up its doors and was famously known as the largest McDonald's restaurant in the world during the 70s and 80s? Yes, our tiny Rock had the largest McDonald's restaurant in the world. It's understandable - you would have to be able to serve the large families who averaged around 4-5 or more kids with seating capacity. Fast food chains took us out of the home cooked meals from home and changed our taste buds from steamed rice to french fried potatoes. The Big Mac ruled over your home made dishes and the usual family gatherings at dinner tables. I don't think Nana was very pleased over our red-white and blue transition into the American lifestyle.

4

Tourism - We're Not the Foreigners Anymore

otel Row along the coastal waters of Tumon Bay with Two Lovers Point in the far right.

On our island of Guam, we nearly import rather than export a vast majority of goods and services. We live off the land more on recreational activities than on gross manufactured products. Seafood is cheaper as we harvest from the ocean locally, but we consume it as soon as we bring it in, so it's fresh. So what exactly is our biggest industry? Tourism. Guam is a popular vacation destination and it consists largely of the following data by volume and country of visitors. Depicted below per the local Guam Visitors Bureau data (pre-Covid era around September 2021). Don't worry, as we progress in post-Covid, I am sure those numbers will climb back up, if not even more. Russian tourists have already started to appear on our shores within the last

15 years. When that happened, the running joke was the saying " The Russians Are Coming! The Russians Are Coming!" as in the 1966 film title

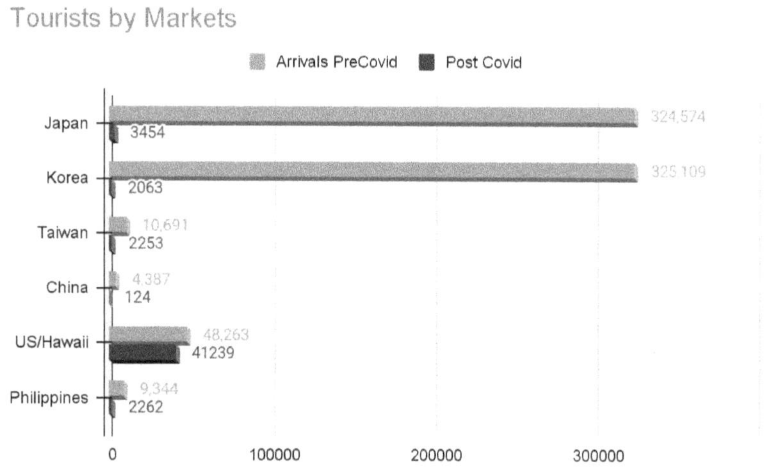

We're a tour package dream for those traveling on a budget because we're practically duty-free, thanks to our territorial and non-state status. There is no state tax applied to your spending. Our location is a short plane ride over from Asia and offers the same amenities and tourist traps of the 50th State. Guam is considered "the poor man's Hawaii." LOL! We guarantee we will give you more bang for your buck. We have the following points of interest and charm that draw the world's curiosity, to name a few.

World-renowned beaches famous for perfect water temperature and unchallenged wonders of sea life for snorkeling and deep-sea diving along with 32 waterfalls and the highest mountain on earth, Mount LamLam ("Lightning") -its height is measured from the base of the deepest part of the ocean - the Marianas Trench

The Marianas Trench

- the deepest known part of the Pacific Ocean, is legendary for its claim in ocean depth. Often recalled in two National Geographic specials, its moniker "The Challenger Deep" at its southern tip, was termed by serious deep-sea divers. A famous French marine explorer Jacques Cousteau was also lured by the challenge during my youth. He came with his team on the famous Calypso submarine to make the expedition. Cousteau and crew member Falco descended down the trench in a bathyscaphe (a manned submersible vessel) and touched the bottom at 35,798 feet after two attempts. But the world record is held by the Vescovo expedition at 35, 853 feet as the deepest manned sea dive at the southern tip of the Trench back in 1960. In more recent years, famed Hollywood filmmaker of "The Titanic" James Cameron also made the solo descent in more modern equipment and comfort.

Chamorro Village

- Located at Paseo Loop in downtown Hagatna - it offers unique island merchandise and art for sale, along with live bands and featured cultural performances. Wednesday Night Markets are the highlight of midweek events for all locals and tourists alike. The tour buses have reserved parking at the location and they come fully packed with tourists from the hotels. Before the end of the night, food vendors are sold out but tired and happy.

Chamorro Night Wednesday Market - family, food and fun!

<u>Golf courses</u> - just like ones in Maui or Oahu, we have lush greens, swaying palms and blue ocean close by, except the "sand traps" are actual sand from the nearby shore. Oh, and try getting a hole-in-one across an ocean inlet which divides you and the par on the other side.

Two Lovers Point views

<u>Puntan Dos Amantes (Two Lovers Point)</u> - This site boasts a famous folklore from the Spanish era, where two young chamoru lovers (a local boy and a chief's daughter) leapt off a steep cliff to their death to escape capture by a Spanish Captain and his troops because the daughter was "promised" to him in marriage. The lovers were trapped by the edge of the cliff with nowhere to run, as the troops were closing in. Not wanting to be caught, the lovers tied their hair together, joined hands and leapt from the cliff into the ocean below. Their bodies were never recovered or found. It is said that perhaps their remains were swept out to sea and fishermen have claimed they have seen their "image" (silhouettes) amongst the rocks that are at the base of the cliff from time to time in the twilight of dawn

The Chocolate House - where the Spanish Governor took his afternoon "cocoa time" repast.

Plaza de Espana and Latte Stone Park are in the heart of Hagatna, the capital of Guam. These are two points of historical remnants of the Spanish and ancient Chamoru era. The plaza was the location of the Spanish Governor's palace, with Spanish tiled buildings fortified with a gated garrison wall and the Basilica (Spanish Cathedral Church) that make up the palace grounds. Not far away is Latte Stone Park. The latte stone is identified with the indigenous Chamoru. Four or more are lined up in pairs and are like giant chalices carved out of stone, standing about 6-7 feet tall. Historians depict that due to its formation in pairs and the flat surface of the bowl-shaped top, its use may have been to hold up village huts like pillars and elevate it from the dirt or in some cases, the tides from the ocean if living close to the shore

Never to be lacking in any tourist setting, there are lots of shopping along hotel row in Tumon Bay, or the mall and plaza stores with souvenirs and packaged sweets made from fruits or coconuts to enjoy.

the
Plaza

5

Cultural Identification - how we connect no matter the distance, no matter the time

Language
- we have expressive ways of saying things when we are speaking formally, we tend to revert to our native Chamorro dialect but there's a common lingo and then the slang lingo. Take the following popular term for example

- *Lan'a (lan-ya)- a swear word, akin to an expletive expressing mild surprise to utter disgust in regret (common) i.e. - Lan'a, he's so full of himself (wistful tone*
- *Lan'a! (laan-yah!) - used loosely by the younger generation to show intention to dare not "screw around" with him or herself*

*If someone shouts this word at you loudly, better be ready to put your dukes up or jam your butt outta there! Run as fast as your flip flops can carry you until they fly off your feet! Needless to say, many a pair of flip flops have been abandoned and never seen again. *SMH*

Music

we are a conglomeration of all things musical and embrace whatever gives us an earful of pleasure:

- -*traditional songs* in our Chamorro tongue where we sing of folklore and love of the land and sea, mostly sung with longing of yesteryear and nostalgia. For an even more profound effect - after a few shots of tuba moonshine or several cases of beer (hehehe)
- -*island jam* when we play our electric guitars and use melodic rhythms to signify the evening sunset and paradise outlook or as the younger generation calls it - surfer dude or ocean dive blue
- -*world influences* - think reggae, cultural chants, techno, rhythm and blues, country, rock and roll, and even non-English music from Asia like K-Pop and J-Pop. There is no limit, so long as we can groove, we don't judge the genre - everybody has a place on our Rock.

Food

- We can be a melting pot of past, present, and future but our taste buds always bring us back to the memories we hold dear with each bite such as...

- Traditional recipes made in our home, family secret ingredient
- Fiestas - a broader gathering table of everyone bringing their specialty dish (a party or celebratory event), contributing to the fare
- Farmers' markets - a whole cultural journey of various offerings, aside from traditional cuisine, there is an infusion of regional influences such as
- *Filipino* lumpia (egg roll) or pancit noodles (egg or rice-based), Kari-

Kari

- *Korean BBQ*, clear glass noodles called "japchae", Kimchi
- *Japanese* sushi, sashimi, teppanyaki or even mochi ice cream
- *Chinese* sausage - sweet/sour pork, fried rice, chow mein, wonton, abalone soup or even orange chicken
- *Hawaiian* - we share the same love for pineapple, banana, coconut, and mango. Kahlua roasted pig, poi, and the king of all meats - SPAM! This universal delicacy of the islands has a cult following for different variations of flavor - regular, low salt, tabasco flavored, teriyaki, cheese, hot and spicy, etc. For those looking for a healthier option - Turkey Spam. There's no end to this "poor man's ham" for the "poor man's Hawaii"!

6

Stories from My Youth

Nothing for something
    - The carefree times when doing nothing was something - I recall some of the best moments in my life were not doing anything with no purpose or intention. People-watching on the beach was one of my favorite pastimes. I often enjoyed sitting on the sand and just watched people surfing, swimming, or sunbathing. On the island, you could do that and no one made you feel like you were wasting your time. No hustle and bustle, just the ocean breeze, palm trees, and me staring into the clouds or the horizon, waiting for sunset. We have the most vivid sunsets of deep orange, red, and gold. I went to John F. Kennedy High School, which was situated right above the edge of a hill overlooking the crowded hotel row and beaches of Tumon Bay. The view from certain classrooms can be distracting since from the elevation, you can see far out to the horizon of the ocean. During morning breaks or lunch hour, some of us would hang out on the second-floor stairwell, sitting on the rails, playing music on our boom boxes, not saying a word, but just staring out to sea. What more could you ask for? I sure miss doing nothing, because as such, it was something - to me.

Child Labor- a slave to the fiesta kitchens.

-Fiestas (large celebratory parties) are an integral part of the Chamoru culture and lifestyle. It is our way of socializing with family, friends old and new. We celebrate Feast Days of Patrons Saints as a village and every household is hosting a party with heavily laden tables of food. The typical fiesta plate will consist of barbecued pork/beef or short ribs/chicken, Spanish 'red rice' (its deep orange color like paella rice), potato salad and a hot spicy sauce made with lemon juice or cider vinegar mixed with soy sauce, small red Chinese peppers, and white or green onions. We call this table sauce "finadene" (fee-nah-deh-nee) an important component to the chamoru cuisine. I always enjoyed fiestas, but not the preparation part prior to the event. As early as the age of seven, my Nana recruited me into the kitchen and started my "training" as a sous chef. I was to help prepare vegetables, side dishes and assist in the execution of family meals. Imagine, a seven-year old being given a knife to cut, chop, filet or slice. Nana clearly was so determined to "mentor" me, not once did she doubt my ability to handle a sharp object. Gordon Ramsay would have been impressed (or dumbfounded?). Go figure.

Each celebration usually begins a night or two before the actual fiesta day. Women were either stationed at inside or outside kitchens (a standard fixture of many households) cooking various dishes, while the men were normally outdoors at the grills, gathered around the smoking pit with a utensil in one hand and a can of beer in the other. You wouldn't be considered a true chamoru if you didn't have a drink in hand as you grill and sometimes spike the marinade with a little bit of fizz from your beer to liven up the taste buds. LOL! So truthfully, my time as a "sous chef" was not only in my family's kitchen, but in other household kitchens all over the island whenever there was a fiesta celebration. You see, Nana would send me and my younger cousin as "helping hands" in representation of her clan to help the hosting family with their preparations. We weren't sure if we were blood relatives or acquaintances, but if you were sent by Nana, you are to address the hostess as "Auntie" and the host as "Uncle". It wasn't our job to know how we were connected to these households, your hands and labor with Nana's name was enough to do our service and contribute to the table. In the meantime, Nana would be back home, cooking and preparing her dish or specialty to bring later when the fiesta was to start. So I jokingly referred to this assignment as "child labor" because I felt we were being parceled out in our youth to not only assist in the kitchen, but to have an early development as a cook or chef. There *was* an advantage to being in the kitchen of so many families. It was entertaining to listen to the stories or gossip by the adults shared around the kitchen. When the party started, the subject or subjects of some of the "buzz" in the kitchen would arrive and it was all sweet smiles with side glances in their presence. Suffice it to say the *"heat"* in the kitchen was not always from the stove or oven. LOL!

Child labor: Nana's Sous Chefs to Master Chefs

Remember that "crazy....?" - Now I will share with you an unforgettable memory of my early childhood. Even now, I swear it truly happened to me in my life. This impactful experience occurred when I was only six years old, when our family lived in Dad's home village of Sinajana (see-nah-hun-yah).

Toilet shock syndrome

- I was at my neighbor's house being cared for, along with my baby brother. I was six years old, my brother was only two. Lola was our neighbor who watched us one time when my Dad had to be somewhere and could not bring us. On this day, I woke up from our afternoon nap because I needed to go to the bathroom. Everyone else was asleep and the house was quiet. So I crept out of the room and went to the bathroom by the kitchen. I had just opened the door when I saw a dark brown snake's head just starting to elevate from the toilet bowl. I was so shaken with fear that I slammed the thin screened door enough to cause a loud bang when it hit the door frame once I ran away to call Lola. Well, the loud bang woke Lola and she heard me running on the wooden floor towards her room. I quickly told her that I saw a snake in the toilet of their bathroom. Of course, she first thought I must have been mistaken, but after a minute, seeing me scared and begging her to get out of the house, it caused her to go and check the bathroom. While I stayed back on the opposite side of the kitchen, watching her, I was terrified recalling what I had seen. Before she opened the door, she made sure to grab the broom nearby. Slowly, she pulled the door open for a little bit, just wide enough for the broom's bristles to slide through. Then she peeked in, and she widened the door to get enough of a view of the toilet. She poked her head in and looked around, still pushing the broom in front of her as a precaution. But of course, she found nothing and she wrote it off as 'my imagination'. I still think that the loud bang from the door slam may have startled the snake and scared it back down the toilet. It may seem impossible to you, but this was around 1966-1967 and our homes were wooden and elevated with beams from a few feet off the ground like stilts. Any animal or small child can crawl around under the house due to the space it created. The other thing was my neighbor's home had a drain pipe coming from under the house in the area of the bathroom and it submerged into a dense copse of thick bushes. So impossible as it might seem, that incident still haunts my consciousness.

To this day, in any place I lived in, I always keep the toilet seat cover down. My young adult son can attest to this because as a child he noticed that it was only in our house that the toilet seat was closed. At the time when he questioned me, I said I did not find it appropriate in an open position because of what we use it for - poop or pee and who wants to smell that? Later on, I did share with him the true story when he was much older. I did not want him to fear something of my own doing or experience. He had been to Guam by then. Having seen geckos on household walls in relatives' homes, or the giant cockroaches scurrying nearby in outdoor spaces, he understood how true and traumatic that experience was for me as a girl.

*Trivia tidbit: The Brown Tree Snake is just as infamous for causing power outages on the island. Usually after a grid blackout incident, once power was restored and the lights are back up, they've been found electrocuted on the high voltage barbed wire fence surrounding the power plant facilities. By the way - this is the only reference to "Brown" that am not anxious to make a connection to. *wink**

7

Conclusion

Chamorro Pride - A Promise to Return

So there you have all the reflections of my reasons for writing this book. It is not the usual travel book that will be mapped out like a guide, solely made up with lists of attractions, or to give tips and suggestions about Guam. This is more a "homage" to my fellow Chamorros who are spread out from all corners of the world. It is dedicated to those who still do their best to continue traditions, customs to preserve who we are, where we came from and never lose that bond that keeps us tied to this tiny Rock in the Marianas. We can still identify proudly as Pacific Islanders and provide our off-island families a sense of pride and belonging by doing the following.

Speak the Chamorro language. Display your Guam flag or the 671 motifs. Make and share traditional dishes with friends, so they can discover who you truly are. "Broaden your horizons" - the world has yet to fully discover many reasons why we still exist and endured, after all we went through in our historical past. We stand firm in our truths.

In my stateside living, I have met people who have been to Guam because they were either in the military and were stationed there during their tour at one point, or they were teachers who came out on an education/teaching internship. The most common reaction when they discover I'm from Guam is they smile first and then share their memories of when they lived there. It's always laughable when they say -

"You know the craziest things that happened to me was during my time in Guam". They fondly recall how hot and humid it was, but they loved the food, and the beautiful beaches and appreciated the locals. This compliment is especially about fiesta time because of the open invitation to go from house to house during village celebrations, partaking in food and drink. I don't know what they would have thought if they ever knew there were children in the kitchens preparing those delicious plates they were consuming.*smile

This is for all the "Browns" living abroad wherever you are. Some phrases to leave you with, so when you hear them, hopefully, a smile will light up your face and be blessed.

"Hafa Adai - Todo mauleg (Hello, how are you - all is good)"

"Tano y Chamoru (The Land and the People)"

"Where America's Day Begins"

"Si Yu'us Ma'ase (God Bless You)"

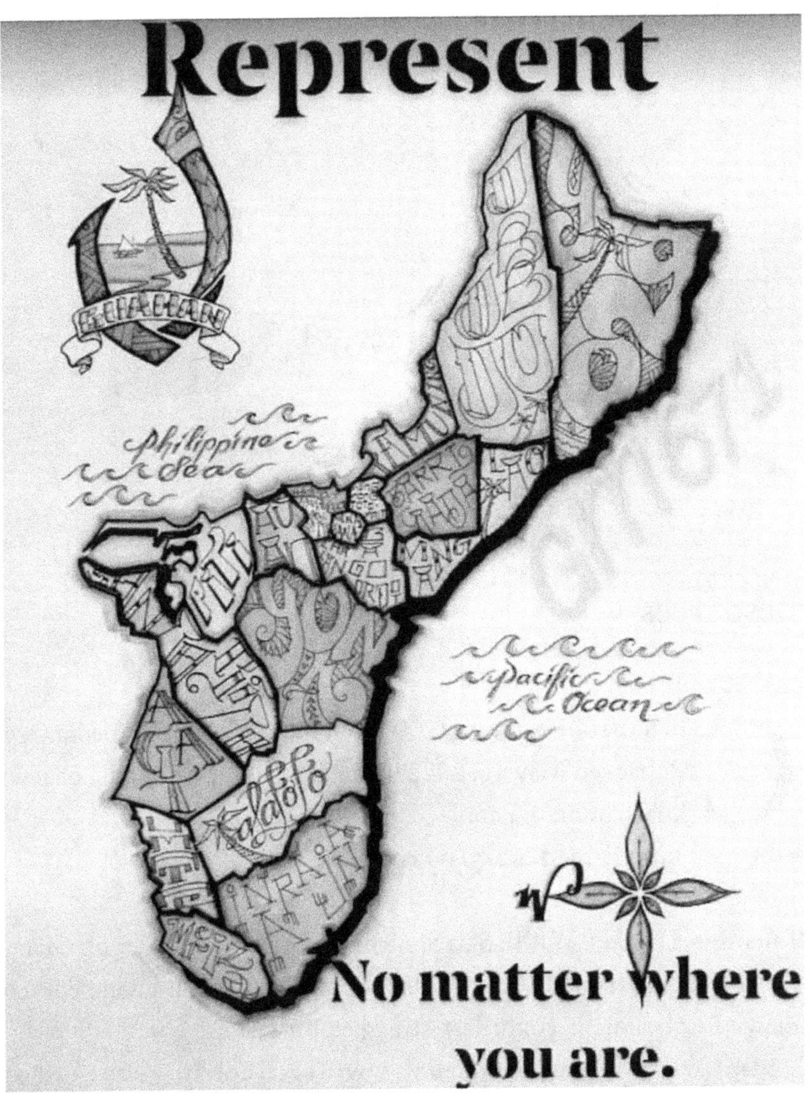

If you enjoyed this book and its contents entertained you, I would appreciate it if you would leave a favorable review on Amazon.

8

Afterword

Resources

Chamorro People. (2004, October 8). Wikipedia.Org. Retrieved May 16, 2022, from https://en.wikipedia.org/wiki/Chamorro_people

https://en.wikipedia.org/wiki/Chamorro_people

Tolentino, D. (n.d.). WWII: Sgt. Shoichi Yokoi, Last Straggler on Guam. Guampedia. Retrieved May 16, 2022, from https://www.guampedia.com/wwii-sgt-shoichi-yokoi-last-straggler-on-guam/

https://www.guampedia.com/wwii-sgt-shoichi-yokoi-last-straggler-on-guam/

Herman, D. (2017, August 15). A Brief, 500-Year History of Guam. Www.Smithsonianmag.Com. Retrieved May 17, 2022, from https://www.smithsonianmag.com/smithsonian-institution/brief-500-year-history-guam-180964508/

Guam's 500 Year History

Richards, L. (2021, June 22). Mariana Trench | In Pursuit of the Abyss. Youtube.Com. Retrieved May 18, 2022, from https://www.youtube.com/watch?v=VoEVezcE0k0

https://www.youtube.com/watch?v=VoEVezcE0k0

Guam Visitors Bureau - Visitor Arrival Statistics. (n.d.). Www.Guamvisitorsbureau.Com. Retrieved May 19, 2022, from https://www.guamvisitorsbureau.com/research/statistics/visitor-arrival-statistics

info@visitguam.org

https://www.guamvisitorsbureau.com/research/statistics/visitor-arrival-statistics

Topping, D. M., Ogo, P. M., & Dungca, B. C. (1980). Chamorro-English Dictionary (PALI Language Texts—Micronesia). University of Hawaii Press.

Wonenberg, B. K. P. F. D. A. (1991). History of the Northern Mariana Islands. In History of the Northern Marianas Islands: Vol. Single (First, Stated ed., pp. 329–335). Public School System Commonwealth of the Northern Mariana Islands.

About the Author

Earlene B. Torres was born in Guam in 1960 and relocated to California in 1980. She has often been mistaken for a Latina or Puerto Rican, to which she proudly announces her Chamorro roots and Pacific Islander heritage. She and her adult son Nicholas currently reside in Clovis, a small city in Fresno county, CA. Earlene has made only five trips back to Guam to visit family in all the years she's been stateside. The one trip she is looking forward to the most is the day she heads back permanently to her beautiful "671 Rock" that her heart has always called *"Home"*.

www.ingramcontent.com/pod-product-compliance
Lightning Source LLC
Chambersburg PA
CBHW060920130726
48001CB00006B/2323